A is for Attitude:
The ABC's of Life

Michelle Frazier Trotman Scott,
Camille Trotman,
Charlean Scott,
and
Tayla Scott
Illustrated by: Morgan Raymore

AuthorHouse™
1663 Liberty Drive
Bloomington, IN 47403
www.authorhouse.com
Phone: 1 (800) 839-8640

Published by AuthorHouse 04/18/2018

ISBN: 978-1-5462-2469-3 (sc)
ISBN: 978-1-5462-2470-9 (e)

Library of Congress Control Number: 2018900548

Print information available on the last page.

This book is printed on acid-free paper.

A is for Attitude:
The ABC's of Life

Acknowledgments

This book has been a long time coming. While growing up, my grandfather, affectionately known as Papa, would always share 'proverbs' that he heard during his youth and they stuck with my siblings and I as we grew into adulthood. As Papa got older, I asked him to share the proverbial sayings with me, but he could only remember one: C is for Cough, its cousin is sneeze. Cover them both with your handkerchief please. As time progressed, I realized that the sayings that he shared were none other than the sayings that appeared in a health ephemera published by the Metropolitan Life Insurance Company in the early 1920's.

Before I knew the sayings were authored by someone else, I declared "I am going to write a book with all of Papa's sayings" because I wanted to share them with my children as well. So, after Papa passed and after some coaxing from my husband, I created my "alphabet proverbs" in 2000. I felt good knowing that I had at least written 'something' down and I went on living.

Fast forward to 2013 - thirteen years after I wrote my first draft of my "alphabet proverbs' book, eleven years after giving birth to my daughter, seven years after getting divorced from her father, and five years after remarrying and gaining two "bonus" daughters; I decided to ask my daughters (biological and bonus) to provide input and made them co-authors of the book. Hence, four authors of the book with myself being the first author, my daughter Camille being the second author, my middle 'bonus' Charlean being the third author, and my oldest 'bonus' Tayla, being the fourth author. I also decided to self-publish the book, but I knew that I needed an illustrator so I prayed and asked for guidance and I waited for God's answer.

Fast forward to 2016, when I realized that my niece, Morgan Sophia was a brilliant illustrator. I asked her if she would be willing to illustrate the book for me, and she was happy to oblige. I sent her a simple text with the following message; *I would like the pictures to represent people of all ages, races, religions, abilities, and genders.* She delivered, and I am more than pleased!

I share all of this to say that I would like to thank Papa for sharing his sayings with me as young girl; Anthony for the encouragement to put words on paper; my mother, Jacqueline for continuing to ask me about the progress of the book; my husband, Scotty for loving me and for giving me my 'bonus' daughters; my daughter Camille, and my 'bonus daughters' Tayla and Charly for providing me with input and confirmation; and to Morgan Sophia for bringing the words to life with her illustrations.

I hope the ABC's of Life bless you as much as they blessed me in both my childhood and adulthood.

Dedication

T his book is dedicated to Robert "Bob" Butler. Thank you for sowing into your family and providing us all with unconditional love. Love you, Papa!

A is for **attitude**; keep it positive all the time. A positive attitude will keep you in line.

B is for the **beauty** that you possess within; inner beauty will always win.

C is for **cough**, its cousin is sneeze; cover them both with your handkerchief please (Metropolitan life Insurance Company, 1920).

D is for the **desire** to be great; being great enhances outstanding traits.

E is for **education**, which is important indeed. A solid education is needed to succeed.

F is for **faith**, which is synonymous with believe; if you keep the faith, you will achieve.

G is for the **grooming** that must be done each day. When you wash, comb and brush, you stay fresh in every way.

H

is for **honest**; it's the right way to be. Being truthful and honest throughout life is key.

I is for the **intelligence** that you exhibit in many ways –
keep doing your best and you'll get better everyday.

J is for the **joy** that you always bring; if you keep joy in your life, you will feel as if you can do anything.

K is for the **kind** words that you should use. Choose your words wisely and it will be hard to loose.

L is for the **love** that we all possess. Show all the love you can and the Creator will do the rest.

M is for the **marvel** of life that you experience each day; when you gaze at the moon, the stars, and the beautiful sun rays.

N is for **neat**, the way you should keep your room. Put away your clothes and toys and make sure you vacuum.

O is for **obedient**, not as difficult as it seems. Obedience brings abundant rewards that you can redeem.

P is for **patience**, a trait that we all need. A person who is patient will most likely succeed.

Q is for the **questions** that you should ask each day.
They will help you understand the things
people do and say.

R is for **respect** - give it, you can't go wrong. If you give respect, you'll get respect your whole life long.

S is for the **scholar** that you most certainly are; your level of knowledge will definitely raise the bar.

T is for the **twinkle** the stars make in the sky. Enjoy the natural beauty created by the Most High.

U is for the **uplift** that's spread with joy and love. When you uplift others, it pleases our Father above.

V is for the **values** that your elders have instilled; to be kind, honest, and respectful and to always do God's will.

W is for the **will** that you have to do your best. If you work hard and remain humble, you will pass life's test.

X is for the **eXceptional** person you have come to be; and since you are a scholar, you know that exceptional begins with 'E'.

Y is for **you**, a very important being, who's a descendant of greatness, including queens and kings.

Z is for the **zenith** of life that you will definitely reach. Set your goals and remain focused and you will feel complete.

Z is for the **zenith** of life that you will definitely reach.
Set your goals and remain focused and you will feel complete.

Y is for **you**, a very important being, who's a descendant of greatness, including queens and kings.

X is for the **eXceptional** person you have come to be. But you are a scholar, you know that exceptional begins with 'E'.

W is for the **will** that you have to do your best. If you work hard and remain humble, you will pass life's test.

Remember to be kind, be honest and respectful to everyone you meet
I promise grandpa

V is for the **values** that your elders have instilled; to be kind, honest, and respectful and to always do God's will.

U is for the **uplift** that's spread with joy and love. When you uplift others, it pleases our Father above.

T is for the **twinkle** the stars make in the sky. Enjoy the natural beauty created by the Most High.

S is for the **scholar** that you most certainly are; your level of knowledge will definitely raise the bar.

R is for **respect** - give it, you can't go wrong. If you give respect, you'll get respect your whole life long.

Q is for the **questions** that you should ask each day.
They will help you understand the things people do and say.

P is for **patience**, a trait that we all need. A person who is patient will most likely succeed.

O is for **obedient**, not as difficult as it seems. Obedience brings abundant rewards that you can redeem.

N is for **neat**, the way you should keep your room. Put away your clothes and toys and make sure you vacuum.

M is for the **marvel** of life that you experience each day; when you gaze at the moon, the stars, and the beautiful sun rays.

L is for the **love** that we all possess. Show all the love you can and the Creator will do the rest.

K is for the **kind** words that you should use. Choose your words wisely and it will be hard to loose.

J is for the **joy** that you always bring; if you keep joy in your life, you will feel as if you can do anything.

I

is for the **intelligence** that you exhibit in many ways – keep doing your best and you'll get better everyday.

H is for **honest**; it's the right way to be. Being truthful and honest throughout life is key.

G is for the **grooming** that must be done each day. When you wash, comb and brush, you stay fresh in every way.

F is for **faith**, which is synonymous with believe; if you keep the faith, you will achieve.

E is for **education**, which is important indeed. A solid education is needed to succeed.

D is for the **desire** to be great; being great enhances outstanding traits.

C is for **cough**, its cousin is sneeze; cover them both with your handkerchief please (Metropolitan Life Insurance Company, 1920).

B is for the **beauty** that you possess within; inner beauty will always win.

A is for **attitude**; keep it positive all the time. A positive attitude will keep you in line.

Dedication

This book is dedicated to Robert "Bob" Butler. Thank you for sowing into your family and providing us all with unconditional love. Love you, Papa!

to illustrate the book for me, and she was happy to oblige. I sent her a simple text with the following message; *I would like the pictures to represent people of all ages, races, religions, abilities, and genders.* She delivered, and I am more than pleased!

I share all of this to say that I would like to thank Papa for sharing his sayings with me as young girl; Anthony for the encouragement to put words on paper; my mother, Jacqueline for continuing to ask me about the progress of the book; my husband, Scotty for loving me and for giving me my 'bonus' daughters; my daughter Camille, and my 'bonus daughters' Tayla and Charly for providing me with input and confirmation; and to Morgan Sophia for bringing the words to life with her illustrations.

I hope the ABC's of Life bless you as much as they blessed me in both my childhood and adulthood.

wanted to share them with my children as well. So, after Papa passed and after some coaxing from my husband, I created my "alphabet proverbs" in 2000. I felt good knowing that I had at least written 'something' down and I went on living.

Fast forward to 2013 - thirteen years after I wrote my first draft of my "alphabet proverbs' book, eleven years after giving birth to my daughter, seven years after getting divorced from her father, and five years after remarrying and gaining two "bonus" daughters; I decided to ask my daughters (biological and bonus) to provide input and made them co-authors of the book. Hence, four authors of the book with myself being the first author, my daughter Camille being the second author, my middle 'bonus' Charlean being the third author, and my oldest 'bonus' Tayla, being the fourth author. I also decided to self-publish the book, but I knew that I needed an illustrator so I prayed and asked for guidance and I waited for God's answer.

Fast forward to 2016, when I realized that my niece, Morgan Sophia was a brilliant illustrator. I asked her if she would be willing

Acknowledgments

This book has been a long time coming. While growing up, my grandfather, affectionately known as Papa, would always share 'proverbs' that he heard during his youth and they stuck with my siblings and I as we grew into adulthood. As Papa got older, I asked him to share the proverbial sayings with me, but he could only remember one: C is for Cough, its cousin is sneeze. Cover them both with your handkerchief please. As time progressed, I realized that the sayings that he shared were none other than the sayings that appeared in a health ephemera published by the Metropolitan Life Insurance Company in the early 1920's.

Before I knew the sayings were authored by someone else, I declared "I am going to write a book with all of Papa's sayings" because I

A is for Attitude:
The ABC's of Life

AuthorHouse™
1663 Liberty Drive
Bloomington, IN 47403
www.authorhouse.com
Phone: 1 (800) 839-8640

Published by AuthorHouse 04/18/2018

ISBN: 978-1-5462-2469-3 (sc)
ISBN: 978-1-5462-2470-9 (e)

Library of Congress Control Number: 2018900548

Print information available on the last page.

This book is printed on acid-free paper.

A is for Attitude:
The ABC's of Life

Michelle Frazier Trotman Scott,
Camille Trotman,
Charlean Scott,
and
Tayla Scott
Illustrated by: Morgan Raymore